Rectangle with Fringe

APPROXIMATE SIZE: 22" x 38" (including fringe)

TOOLS: Size Q crochet hook

GAUGE: 5 sc = 4"

STITCHES: Single crochet (sc)

WIDTH OF STRIPS: 2"

COLOR	FABRIC YARDAGE
Dark Blue	2⅔ yards (96" wide)
Yellow & White Pattern	2⅔ yards (96" wide)
White	2⅔ yards (96" wide)
Blue Multi	2⅔ yards (96" wide)

NOTE: Work in the back loop of stitches throughout. Rug is worked in rows out from center foundation chain. Change colors for each row. Each row requires approximately ¾ yards of fabric. Leave 3" of each strip unworked at each end of each row for fringe.

Rectangle with Fringe rug created by Janice Besinger.

INSTRUCTIONS

Beginning 3" from end of first strip, chain 51. Fasten off, leaving 3" tail. This is the center row of the rug.

Row 1: With another color, begin 3" from end of strip, work 2 sc in the first ch, sc in each ch across, work 2 sc in last ch. Fasten off, leaving 3" tail.

Row 2: With another color, begin 3" from end of strip and work 2 sc in back loop of first sc of Row 1, sc in the back loop of each sc across, work 2 sc in the back loop of the last sc. Fasten off, leaving a 3" tail.

Rows 3–10: Work as for Row 2. Turn to work across remaining side of foundation chain.

Rows 11–20: Repeat Rows 1–10.

Fringe: Cut remaining strips into 7" lengths. Across end, hold 2 strips together and make a lark's head knot in each end stitch of each row. Across side, use 2 strips to make 2 knots in corners. Use 2 strips to make a knot in next stitch. Make knots with a single strip in each of the next 2 stitches. Alternate 2-strip knots and 1-strip knots in every 2 stitches across.

Lark's Head Knot

Fold strip in half. Pull loop up through a stitch on last row.

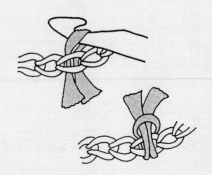

Pull ends of strip through loop. Pull ends firmly.

Rag Rugs

2nd Edition, Revised and Expanded

2nd Edition, Revised and Expanded

Rag Rugs

16 Easy Crochet Projects to Make with Strips of Fabric

Suzanne McNeill

Design Originals

an Imprint of Fox Chapel Publishing

www.d-originals.com

ISBN 978-1-57421-918-0

Heart with Twisted Loop Border rug on front cover by Sara Quintana.

© 2006, 2014 by Suzanne McNeill and New Design Originals Corporation, *www.d-originals.com*, an imprint of Fox Chapel Publishing, 800-457-9112, 1970 Broad Street, East Petersburg, PA 17520. *Rag Rugs, 2nd Edition, Revised and Expanded* (ISBN 978-1-57421-918-0, 2014) is a completely revised and expanded second edition, featuring full-color photography, of *Rag Rugs* (ISBN 978-1-57421-267-9, 2006), published by Design Originals.

Printed in the United States of America
Second printing

12

14

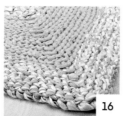
16

18

CONTENTS

20

22

24

26

28

32

34

36

38

40

44

46

History

In 1949, the oldest surviving rug was discovered in Siberia. Russian archaeologist Sergei Rudenko unearthed the rug, known as the "Pazyryk carpet," which had been frozen since the fifth century BCE. This well-preserved rug still had color and its design was mostly intact, with an average of 200 knots per square inch.

The ancient art of carpet weaving, particularly Persian and Oriental rugs, reached its height in Turkey and Central Asia in the sixteenth century. Outstanding examples of artistic handmade rugs were created in France and England in the seventeenth and eighteenth centuries. Today, Native American rug makers in the southwestern part of the United States continue the rug-making craft begun by their ancestors in the early eighteenth century.

All rugs were handmade until 1839, when Erastus Bigelow introduced the power loom. By 1850, his power loom had tripled rug production. Over the years and in many cultures, rugs have been fabricated from wool, velvet, chenille, rags, straw, and fiber.

Ever since Aladdin captured our imagination with his flying carpet, and rugs were prized possessions in mighty castles and humble cottages, handmade rugs have held their appeal. Take part in this time-honored tradition and create your own crochet rag rug to enjoy in your home or to give as a special gift sure to be cherished for years!

Materials

Rag rug projects require only cotton or cotton/polyester blend fabric and large crochet hooks. The supplies are inexpensive and can be found at your local craft, fabric, or variety store. Visit a consignment shop to discover vintage tablecloths or curtains that can be recycled into today's beautiful crochet rug. Even old sheets from the linen closet can be cut up to make great rugs. Mix prints and patterns, brights and pastels, to create rugs that enhance the décor of any room. Have fun and exercise your imagination!

Your fabric stash can become a beautiful crochet rug!

Basic Tips

The Original Recycling Project!

Crochet homespun heirlooms. Simply crochet strips of multicolored fabrics on a large crochet hook to create lovely accents for your home.

BASIC MATERIALS

- Assorted fabrics (100% cotton or polyester/cotton blends)
- Outgrown clothing and sheets are also suitable
- Size Q crochet hook
- Scissors
- Safety pins

Strips. Fold fabric in half. Clip folded edge. Rip fabric. To join strips, sew, knot, or tie ends together. Roll strips into a ball. Alternatively, you can cut the fabric with scissors or a rotary cutting tool. *Note:* Depending on how wide you cut your strips, your finished rug may end up smaller or larger than the pattern states. Simply add more rows to the design, if your rug is falling short of the finished size estimate of the pattern.

Joining Strips. Sew across ends of strips, if desired. Knot ends and leave ends free for a shaggy look. Or, cut a slit in the end of each strip. Pull one strip through slits.

Chain Stitch (ch). Tie a slip knot in a fabric end (this counts as the first ch st). Insert hook through loop. Yarn over hook, pull a loop through (A). Repeat for the desired number of chs (B).

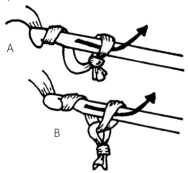

Single Crochet (sc). Insert hook in second ch from hook (A). Yarn over hook, draw up a loop – two loops on hook. Yarn over hook, draw loop through both loops on hook (B). Sc completed (C).

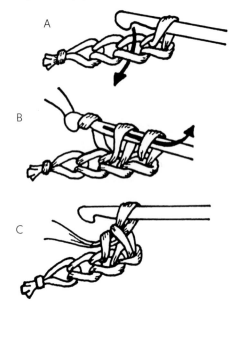

Double Crochet (dc). Yarn over hook, insert hook in third ch from hook (A). Yarn over hook, pull up loop – third loops on hook. Yarn over hook, pull through two loops (B). Yarn over hook, pull through last two loops on hook (C).

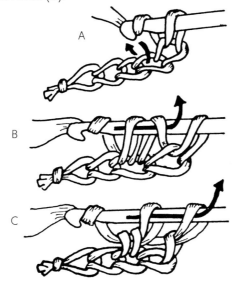

Slip Stitch (sl st). Insert hook in st, yarn over hook, pull up through st, and loop on hook.

Changing Colors. Work last yarn over hook with new color. Pull through last two loops of stitch. Lay ends of both colors across top of row and work next several stitches over ends to secure.

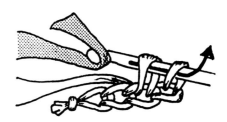

Finish Edge. Make increases in stitches at each end to ensure that rug lies flat. If the edge ruffles, too many stitches have been added. Remove some stitches. If the edge pulls under, add more stitches.

Oval with Fringe

APPROXIMATE SIZE: 26" x 38" (including fringe)

TOOLS: Size Q crochet hook

GAUGE: 2 sc = 2"

STITCHES: Single crochet (sc)

WIDTH OF STRIPS: 2½"

COLOR	FABRIC YARDAGE
Green & White Stripe	2⅔ yards (96" wide)
Dark Blue	2⅔ yards (96" wide)
Light Blue	2⅔ yards (96" wide)
Green	2 yards (96" wide)

INSTRUCTIONS

Chain 20, starting with green and white stripe.

Rnd 1 (Green/white stripe): Sc in second ch from hook and in each ch to end. Work 5 sc in last ch. Turn to work across remaining side of foundation chain. Sc in each ch to end. Work 5 sc in loop of turning chain.

Rnd 2 (Green): Sc in each sc to end, work 2 sc in each sc around end. Turn to work across other side, sc to end. Make 2 sc in each sc around end.

Rnds 3–12: Work as for Rnd 2, making increases in stitches at each end to make rug lie flat. Fasten off at the end of Rnd 12.

Rnd 3 (Green/white stripe)

Rnd 4 (Dark blue)

Rnd 5 (Green/white stripe)

Rnd 6 (Light blue)

Rnd 7 (Dark blue)

Rnd 8 (Green/white stripe)

Rnd 9 (Green)

Rnd 10 (Green/white stripe)

Rnd 11 (Light blue)

Rnd 12 (Dark blue)

Fringe: Cut remaining strips into 7" lengths. Working around end of rug, hold 3 strips together. Make a lark's head knot in 1 stitch of last round. Repeat in the next stitch. Use 1 strip to make a knot in the next stitch. Alternate 3-strip knot in 2 stitches, and a single-strip knot in 1 stitch around both ends of rug. Across sides, alternate two 3-strips knots with one 2-strip knot.

Oval with Fringe rug created by Janice Besinger.

Lark's Head Knot

Fold strip in half. Pull loop up through a stitch on last row.

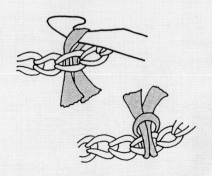

Pull ends of strip through loop. Pull ends firmly.

Pastel Heart

APPROXIMATE SIZE: 33" x 24"

TOOLS: Size Q crochet hook, safety pins

GAUGE: 3 sl st = 2"

STITCHES: Slip stitch (sl st)

WIDTH OF STRIPS: 2"

COLOR	FABRIC YARDAGE
Blue Pattern	1 yard (44" wide)
Green	4½ yards (44" wide)
Multicolor Stripe	3 yards (44" wide)

Pastel Heart rug
created by
Kathy E. Hellems.

INSTRUCTIONS

Chain 21.

Rnd 1 (Blue pattern): Sl st in second ch from hook and in each of the next 9 ch. Skip next ch, sl st in next ch. (Mark this stitch with a safety pin for center top). Sl st in each ch to end. Work 3 sl st in last ch. Turn to work across remaining side of foundation chain. Sl st in each of the next 9 ch, work 3 sl st in next ch. (Mark the center stitch of this group for center bottom). Sl st in each ch to end. Work 3 sl st in ch – 1 loop at end.

Rnd 2 (Green): Sl st in each sl st to top center stitch, skip this stitch, sl st in next sl st. (Move pin to mark this stitch). Sl st in each sl st to end, work 2 sl st in each of the 3 sl st around end, sl st in each sl st to center bottom, work 3 sl st in this stitch. (Move pin to mark center stitch). Sl st in each sl st to end, work 2 sl st in each sl st around end.

Rnds 3–10: Work as for Rnd 2, skipping the center top stitch, working 3 sl st in the center bottom and making increases in stitches at each end to ensure that rug lies flat. Fasten off at the end of Rnd 10.

Rnds 3–7 (Green)

Rnds 8–10 (Multicolor stripe)

Long Oval Runner

APPROXIMATE SIZE: 16" x 51"

TOOLS: Size Q crochet hook

GAUGE: 3 dc = 2"

STITCHES: Double crochet (dc)

WIDTH OF STRIPS: 2"

COLOR	FABRIC YARDAGE
Tan Print	2 yards (44" wide)
Light Green	2 yards (44" wide)
Dark Brown	2⅔ yards (96" wide)
Blue	2⅔ yards (96" wide)
Lighter Brown	2⅔ yards (96" wide)
Green Print	2⅔ yards (96" wide)
Dark Green	2⅔ yards (96" wide)

INSTRUCTIONS

Chain 50.

Rnd 1 (Tan print): Dc in third ch from hook and in each ch to end. Work 6 dc in last ch. Turn to work across remaining side of foundation chain. Dc in each ch to end. Work 6 dc in loop of turning chain.

Rnd 2 (Light green): Ch 2, dc in each dc to end, work 2 dc in each dc around end. Turn to work across other side and dc in each dc to end. Work 3 dc in each dc around end.

Rnd 3 (Dark brown): Ch 2, dc in each dc to end, work, 2 dc in next dc, dc in next dc. Alternate 2 dc with next dc, dc in next dc around end. Dc across other side to end. Work 2 dc in next dc, dc in next dc around end as before.

Rnds 4–7: Work as for Rnd 3, making increases in stitches at each end to make rug lie flat. Fasten off at the end of Rnd 8.

Rnd 4 (Blue)

Rnd 5 (Lighter brown)

Rnd 6 (Green print)

Rnd 7 (Dark green)

Long Oval Runner rug created by Janice Besinger.

Multicolor Heart

APPROXIMATE SIZE: 34" x 31"

TOOLS: Size Q crochet hook, safety pins

GAUGE: 3 sc = 2"

STITCHES: Single crochet (sc)

WIDTH OF STRIPS: 2"

COLOR	FABRIC YARDAGE
Assorted prints & solids	15 total yards (44" wide)

NOTE: Work in the back loop of stitches throughout.

INSTRUCTIONS

Chain 43.

Rnd 1: Sc in second ch from hook and in each of the next 19 chs. Skip 3 ch, sc in next ch. (Mark this stitch with a safety pin for top center). Sc in each of the next 19 ch to end. Work 3 sc in last ch. Turn to work across remaining side of foundation chain. Sc in each of the next 20 ch, work 3 sc in the next ch. (Mark the center stitch of this group for bottom center). Sc in each ch to end. Work 3 sc in loop of turning chain.

Rnd 2: Ch 1, sc in each sc to within 1 stitch of top center, skip 3 sc, sc in next sc. (Move pin to make this stitch). Sc in each sc to 3-sc group at end. Work 2 sc in each sc around end. Sc in each sc to bottom center, work 3 sc in this sc. (Move pin to center sc of third group). Sc in each sc to end, work 2 sc in each sc around end.

Rnds 3–14: Work as for Rnd 2, skipping 3 stitches at the center top on each round and adding stitches at each end and at center bottom. Make increase stitches at each end to make rug lie flat. Fasten off at the end of Rnd 14.

Multicolor Heart
rug created by
Jan Werner.

Shaggy Oval

APPROXIMATE SIZE: 22" x 34"

TOOLS: Size Q crochet hook

GAUGE: 2 dc = 2"

STITCHES: Double crochet (dc)

WIDTH OF STRIPS: 2"

COLOR	FABRIC YARDAGE
Assorted Prints & Solids	12 total yards (44" wide)

NOTE: To join strips, knot ends together, leaving 2" tails.

INSTRUCTIONS

Chain 11.

Rnd 1: Dc in third ch from hook dc in each ch to end. Work 3 dc in last ch. Turn to work across remaining side of foundation chain. Dc in each ch to end. Work 3 dc in ch-2 loop at end.

Rnd 2: Ch 2, dc in each dc across to end, work 2 dc in each dc around end, turn to work across other side, dc in each dc to end, work 2 dc in each dc around end.

Rnds 3–10: Work as for Rnd 2, making increases in stitches at each end to insure that rug lies flat. Fasten off at the end of Rnd 10.

Shaggy Oval
rug created by
Deborah Wehunt Adams.

Long Oval with Shell Border

APPROXIMATE SIZE: 22" x 46"

TOOLS: Size Q crochet hook

GAUGE: 2 sc = 2"

STITCHES: Single crochet (sc), Double crochet (dc), Half Double crochet (hdc)

WIDTH OF STRIPS: 2½"

COLOR	FABRIC YARDAGE
Light Blue	2½ yards
Light Blue Print	3 yards
White	4½ yards
Medium Blue Print	4 yards
Yellow	2¼ yards
Dark Blue	1½ yards

NOTE: Work in the back loop of stitches throughout. Work in both loops for last round.

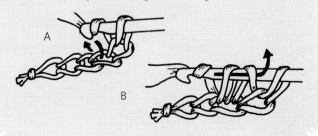

Long Oval with Shell Border rug created by Deb Seda-Testut.

INSTRUCTIONS

Chain 30.

Rnd 1 (Light blue): 6 sc in second ch from hook (working one side of the foundation chain). Sc in each ch across, 6 sc in last ch. Turn, work sc in each ch across (working in opposite side of foundation ch) sl st to first sc.

Sc in second ch from hook in each ch to end. Work 6 sc in last ch. Turn to work across remaining side of foundation chain. Sc in each ch to end. Work 6 sc in loop of turning chain.

Rnd 2 (Light blue print): Sc in each sc to end, work 2 sc in each of the 6 sc around end. Turn to work across other side and sc to end. Work 2 sc in each sc around end.

Rnd 3: (Light blue print) Repeat Rnd 2 (increase rnd).

Rnd 4: (Dark blue) Repeat Rnd 2 (increase rnd).

Rnd 5: (White) Repeat Rnd 2 (increase rnd).

Rnds 6–7: (Medium blue print) Sc in each sc around (work even).

Rnd 8: (Yellow) Repeat Rnd 2 (increase rnd).

Rnd 9: (Light blue) Repeat Rnd 6 (work even).

Rnd 10: (Medium blue print) Repeat Rnd 2 (increase rnds).

Rnd 11: (Yellow) Repeat Rnd 2 (increase rnds).

Rnd 12: (White) Ch 2, 2 dc, 1 hdc in same stitch, * sk 1 sc, sl st in next sc, sk sc, (1 hdc, 2 dc, 1 hdc) in next sc repeat from * around ending with a sl in the ch2.

Fasten off. Weave in ends.

Half Double Crochet (hdc)

Yarn over, insert hook in st or ch (A).
Yarn over, pull up loop—3 loops on hook.
Yarn over, pull through all 3 loops on hook (B).

Rectangle

APPROXIMATE SIZE: 36" x 46"

TOOLS: Size Q crochet hook

GAUGE: 3 dc = 3"

STITCHES: Double crochet (dc), Single crochet (sc)

WIDTH OF STRIPS: 2"

COLOR	FABRIC YARDAGE
Assorted Prints & Solids	32 total yards (44" wide)

INSTRUCTIONS

Chain 12.

Rnd 1: Dc in third ch from hook dc in each ch to end. Work 4 dc n last ch. Turn to work across remaining side of foundation chain. Dc in each ch to end. Work 4 dc in loop of turning chain.

Rnd 2: Dc in each dc to end, work 3 dc in first dc of 4 – dc group at end (corner), dc in each of the 2 center dc, work 3 dc in next dc (corner), dc in each dc across other side to end, work 3 dc in first dc of 4 – dc group at end (corner), dc in each of the 2 center dc, work 3 dc in last dc (corner).

Rnd 3: Dc in each dc across to end, work 3 dc in center dc of next corner, dc in each dc across to center dc of next corner, work 3 dc in center dc of corner, dc in each dc across end, work 3 dc in center dc of last corner, dc in each dc across end, work 3 dc in center dc of last corner.

Rnds 4–17: Work as for Rnd 3, making 3 dc in the center dc of each corner group on the previous row.

Rnd 18: Ch 1, sc in each dc around, working 3 sc in the center stitch of each corner group. Fasten off.

Rectangle rug created by Jan Werner.

Beginner Blocks

APPROXIMATE SIZE: 31" x 38"

TOOLS: Size Q crochet hook, rug needle

GAUGE: 2 sc = 2"

STITCHES: Chain stitch (ch), Slip stitch (sl st), Single crochet (sc), Half double crochet (hdc), Double crochet (dc)

WIDTH OF STRIPS: 2¼"

COLOR	FABRIC YARDAGE
Print	6 yards
Green	3 yards
Purple	9¾ yards

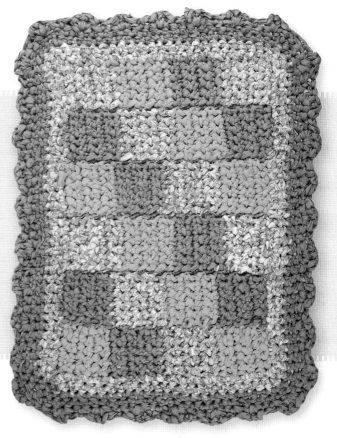

Beginner Blocks
rug created by
Deborah Wehunt Adams.

INSTRUCTIONS

Begin Panels 1 & 4: Make 2 with Green, ch 6.

Row 1: Work sc in 2nd ch from hook and each ch across – 5 sc. Ch 1, turn. (Note: Mark first row as top of panel.)

Rows 2–6: Sc in first sc and each sc across – 5 sc. Ch 1 turn. At end of last row, do not ch 1, turn. Attach Print in last sc. Fasten off Green.

Rows 7–12: Sc in first sc and each sc across – 5 sc. Ch 1 turn. At end of last row, do not ch 1, turn. Attach Purple in last sc. Fasten off Print. Ch 1, turn.

Rows 13–18: Sc in first sc and each sc across – 5 sc. Ch 1 turn. At end of last row, do not ch 1, turn. Attach Green in last sc. Fasten off Purple. Chain 1, turn.

Rows 19–24: Sc in first st and each st across – 5 sc. Ch 1 turn. At end of last row, do not ch 1, turn. Fasten off Green.

Beginner Blocks *(continued)*

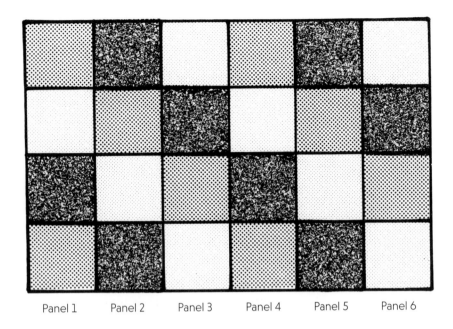

Panel 1 Panel 2 Panel 3 Panel 4 Panel 5 Panel 6

Panels 2 & 5: Repeat Rows 1–6 with Purple. Repeat Rows 7–12 with Green. Repeat Rows 13–18 with Print. Repeat Rows 19–24 with Purple.

Panels 3 & 6: Repeat Rows 1–6 with Print. Repeat Rows 7–12 with Purple. Repeat Rows 13–18 with Green. Repeat Rows 19–24 with Print.

Assembly: Whipstitch panels together as illustrated, with all marked edges at the top.

Whipstitch

With right sides facing, align rows or stitches of pieces to be joined. Insert needle through a back loop of each piece. Insert needle through back loops on next stitches or rows (A). For squares, join center stitches of corners (B).

A   B

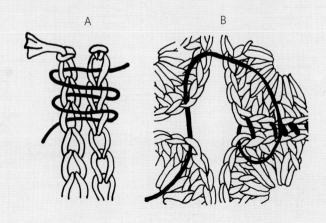

Half Double Crochet (hdc)

Yarn over, insert hook in st or ch (A).
Yarn over, pull up loop—3 loops on hook.
Yarn over, pull through all 3 loops
on hook (B).

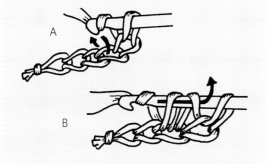

Edging: Attach Print in upper right corner in end of Row 1, just before first stitch on top row.

Rnd 1: Ch 1, work 3 sc for corner in same space as joining, *sc in next 36 sc, work 3 sc in next row end on side edge for next corner; work 22 sc evenly spaced in row ends across side to last row end, * work 3 sc in last row end for corner. Repeat from * to * around. Join with sl st in top of beginning ch-1.

Rnd 2: Work as for Rnd 1, sc in each sc around, making 3 sc in center of each 3-sc corner group – 136 sc. Join. Attach Purple in last stitch. Fasten off Print.

Rnd 3: Ch 1, sc in same sc, 3 sc in next st for corner, sc in each sc around, working 3 sc in center sc of each 3-sc corner group – 144 sc. Join as before.

Rnd 4: Work another row of Purple – 152 sc.

Rnd 5—Shell Border: Ch 1. *skip 1 sc, all in next sc work hdc, 2 dc, hdc (shell formed). Skip 1 sc, sc in next sc. Repeat from * around to make 38 shells. Sl st to top of beginning ch-1 to join. Fasten off, weave in ends.

Small Rectangle

APPROXIMATE SIZE: 23" x 30"

TOOLS: Size Q crochet hook, rug needle

GAUGE: 4 sc = 3"

STITCHES: Chain st (ch), Slip stitch (sl st), Single crochet (sc)

WIDTH OF STRIPS: 2¼"

COLOR	FABRIC YARDAGE
Gray Print	7 yards
Light Purple	4¾ yards
Dark Purple	3½ yards

Small Rectangle
rug created by
Sara Quintana.

INSTRUCTIONS

Begin: Gray Print, ch 15.

Rnd 1: Sc in 2nd ch from hook, sc in each of the next 12 ch, 3 sc in last chain, sc in next 12 ch on the other side of foundation chain, 2 sc in last ch. Join with a sl st.

Rnd 2: Ch 1 (first sc), 2 sc in same stitch as ch-1, sc in next 12 sc, 3 sc in next sc (for corner), sc in next sc, 3 sc in next sc (for corner), sc in the next 12 sc, 3 sc in next sc, (for corner), sc in next sc. Join.

Rnd 3: Ch 1, 3 sc in next sc, *sc in next 14 sc, 3 sc in center sc of corner 3-sc group, sc in next 3 sc, 3 sc in center sc of corner 3-sc group. *Repeat from * to *. Sc in next 2 sc. Join to top of beginning ch-1.

Rnd 4: Ch 1, work 3 sc in next sc, *sc in each sc across to center sc of corner group, work 3 sc in this sc, sc in each sc across to center sc of next corner work 3 sc in the sc*. Repeat from * to *. Sc in each sc across end.

Rnds 5–8: Work as for Rnd 4 with Gray Print.

Rnds 9–10: Work as for Rnd 4 with Light Purple.

Rnds 11–13: Work as for Rnd 4 with Dark Purple.

Rnd 14: Work as for Rnd 4 with Light Purple.

Rnds 15–16: Work as for Rnd 4 with Gray Print.

Rnd 17: Work as for Rnd 4 with Light Purple. Fasten off. Weave in end.

Large Rectangle with Shell Border

APPROXIMATE SIZE: 44" x 32"

TOOLS: Size P crochet hook, rug needle

GAUGE: 3 sc = 2"

STITCHES: Chain stitch (ch), Slip stitch (sl st), Single crochet (sc), Half double crochet (hdc), Double crochet (dc)

WIDTH OF STRIPS: 2"

COLOR	FABRIC YARDAGE
Large Fruit Print	5 yards
White Print	7 yards
Other Fruit Print	4 yards
Blue and Gold Print	11 yards

Large Rectangle with Shell Border rug created by Liz Erickson.

INSTRUCTIONS

Begin: Large Fruit Print, ch 17.

Rnd 1: Sc in 2nd ch from hook, sc in each of the next 14 ch, 3 sc in last chain, sc in next 14 stitches across other side of foundation chain, 2 sc in last ch. Join to beginning ch of row.

Rnd 2: Ch 1 (first sc), work 2 sc in same stitch as ch-1, sc in next 15 sc, 3 sc in next sc (for corner), sc in next sc, 3 sc in next sc (for corner), sc in the next 14 sc, 3 sc in next sc, (for corner), sc in next sc. Join.

Rnd 3: Ch 1, work 3 sc in next sc, *sc in each sc across to center sc of corner group, 3 sc in this sc (for corner), sc across to center sc of corner group, 3 sc in sc. * Repeat from * to *. Sc in each sc across end. Join.

Rnds 4–7: Repeat Rnd 3, adding 2 sc on sides and ends between corners. Continue to put 3 sc in corners. Fasten off Large Fruit Print.

Rnds 8–12: Work as for Rnd 3 with White Print.

Rnds 13–15: Work as for Rnd 3 with Other Fruit Print.

Rnds 16–18: Work as for Rnd 3 with White Print.

Rnds 19–22: Work as for Rnd 3 with Blue and Gold Print. Do not fasten off.

Shell Border: With Blue and Gold Print, ch 1, * sc in next sc, hdc in next sc, work 2 dc in next sc, hdc in next sc*. Repeat * to * around – 50 shells. Work 3 stitches in each corner sc. Join. Fasten off. Weave in end.

Half Double Crochet (hdc)

Yarn over, insert hook in st or ch (A).
Yarn over, pull up loop—3 loops on hook.
Yarn over, pull through all 3 loops
on hook (B).

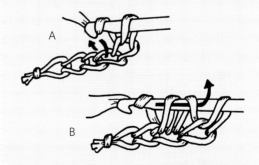

Granny Squares

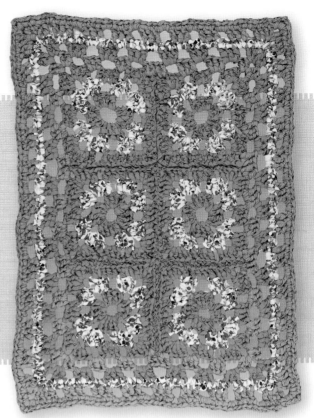

APPROXIMATE SIZE: 28" x 36"

TOOLS: Size P crochet hook, rug needle

GAUGE: each square approx. 9" across

STITCHES: Chain stitch (ch), Slip stitch (sl st), Single crochet (sc), Double crochet (dc)

WIDTH OF STRIPS: 1⅛"

COLOR	FABRIC YARDAGE
Print	3¾ yards
Tan	2¼ yards
Teal	6¾ yards

Granny Squares rug created by Deb Seda-Testut.

INSTRUCTIONS

Square: (Make 6) With Print, ch 8 and close into a ring with sl st in first ch.

Note: Ch 3 at the beginning of each round (counts as 1st dc).

Rnd 1: Ch 3, 3 dc in ring, ch 3, work (4 dc in ring, ch 3) 3 times. Join with sl st in top of beginning ch-3. Fasten off.

Rnd 2: Attach Teal in any ch-3 loop. (Ch 3, 2 dc, ch 3, 3 dc) in corner loop, dc in next dc, ch 2, skip 2 dc, dc in next dc, *work (3 dc, ch 3, 3 dc) in corner loop, dc in next dc, ch 2, skip 2 dc, dc in next dc*. Repeat from * to * around. Join. Fasten off.

Rnd 3: Attach Print in any ch-3 corner loop. (Ch 3, 2 dc, ch 3, 3 dc) in corner loop, dc in next dc, ch 2, skip 2 dc, dc in next dc, 2 dc in next space, dc in next dc, ch 2 skip 2 dc, dc in next dc, *(3 dc, ch 3, 3 dc) in corner loop, dc in next dc, ch 2, skip 2 dc, dc in next dc, 2 dc in next space, dc in next dc, ch 2 skip 2 dc, dc in next dc*. Repeat from * to * around. Join. Fasten off.

Assembly: Sew squares together, matching sts and using the back loop only of each stitch in Rnd 4. Join squares 3 wide by 2 high.

Border: Work with right side facing you.

Rnd 1: Attach Tan in any corner, ch 3, 1 dc, ch 2, 2 dc, in same space (beg corner made), *ch 2, skip next 3 stitches, 3 dc in next ch-2 space, repeat from * to next Seamed corner space, 2 dc in each seamed corner space, repeat from * to next corner; (2 dc, ch 2, 2 dc) in corner space, continue in pattern around, end with sl st in 3rd ch of beginning ch-3. Fasten off.

Rnd 2: Attach Teal to any corner, ch 3, 1 dc, ch 2, 2 dc, in same space (beg corner made), *ch 2, skip next 3 stitches, 3 dc in ch-2 sp, repeat from * to next corner (2 dc, ch 2, 2 dc) in corner space, ch 2, sk next 3 sts, 3 dc in ch-2 space, repeat from * to next corner (2 dc, ch 2, 2 dc) in corner space, continue in pattern around.

Rnd 3: Attach Print in any corner, ch 1, 2 sc, ch 2, 2 sc in same space, sc in next 2 stitches, *2 sc in ch-2 space, sc in next 3 stitches, repeat from * to next corner, (2 sc, ch 2, 2sc) in corner space, continue in pattern around ending with sl st to 3rd ch of beginning ch-3. Fasten off.

Rnd 4: Attach Tan in any corner, ch 3, 1 dc, ch 2, 2 dc in same space, dc in next 2 sts, *3 dc in ch-2 space, ch 2, skip next 3 stitches, repeat from * to next corner, (2 dc, ch 2, 2 dc) in corner space, dc in next 2 stitches, continue in pattern around ending with sl st to 3rd ch of beginning ch-3. Fasten off. Weave in all ends.

To Form a Ring

Make a chain. Insert hook in first ch (A).
Pull through ch st and loop on hook (B).

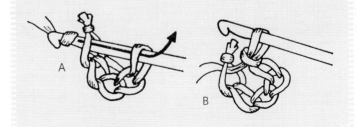

Star

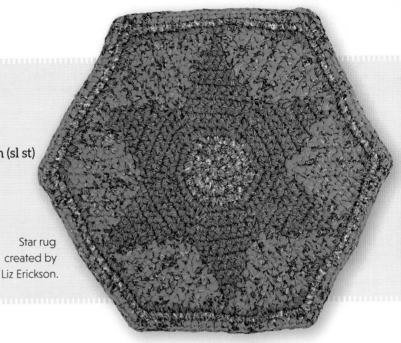

APPROXIMATE SIZE: 29" across points

TOOLS: Size P crochet hook

GAUGE: 3 sc = 2"

STITCHES: Chain stitch (ch), Single crochet (sc), Slip stitch (sl st)

WIDTH OF STRIPS: 1⅛"

COLOR	FABRIC YARDAGE
Large Orange Flower Print	7 yards
Small Orange Flower Print	2 yards
Turquoise Print	5½ yards

Star rug created by Liz Erickson.

INSTRUCTIONS

Begin: With Small Orange Flower Print, ch 4. Join to form a ring.

Rnd 1: Ch 1, 2 sc in each ch. Join (8 sc).

Rnd 2: Ch 1, 2 sc in each sc around. Join (16 sc).

Rnd 3: Ch 1, *sc in next sc, 2 sc in next sc*. Repeat from * to * around. Join (24 sc).

Rnd 4: Ch 1, *sc in next 3 sc, 2 sc in next sc *. Repeat from * to * around. Join (30 sc). Fasten off Small Orange Flower Print.

Star Points:

Row 1: Attach Turquoise Print in a sc. Ch 1, sc in next 5 sc, ch 1, turn.

Row 2: Sc in next 4 sc, 2 sc in last sc, ch 1, turn (6 sc).

Row 3: *Sc in each sc, 2 sc in last sc. Ch 1, turn*. Repeat from * to * 2 times to add rows 4 and 5. Ch 1. Turn.

Rows 6–13: **Skip 1 sc. Sc in each of next sc across. Ch 1. Turn**. Repeat from ** to ** until you have only 1 sc left. Fasten off. (Point made.)

Next 4 Points: To attach, sl st in last sc of Row 1 of previous point. Repeat Rows 1 of previous point. Repeat Rows 1 and 2. At the end of Row 2, sl st in end of Row 2 of previous point. Repeat Rows 3 and 4. At the end of Row 4, sl st in the end of Row 4 of previous point. Repeat Rows 5–13 to complete point.

Last Point: Attach and repeat Row 1 as for other points. Sl st in the end of Row 1 of first point. Repeat Rows 2–5. Sl st at the end of each row to the end of the same row on adjacent points. Repeat Rows 6–13 to complete point.

Diamond Filler Blocks:

First Block: With right side facing, attach Large Orange Flower Print to left side of sc (on Row 13) at tip of any star point.

Row 1: Sc in same space as joining. Sl st in ch-1 loop at end of Row 11 of star point. Ch 1, turn.

Row 2: Work 2 sc in sc. Ch 1, turn.

Row 3: Sc in first sc, 2 sc in next sc. Sl st in ch-1 loop of Row 9 of star point. Ch 1, turn.

Row 4: Sc across to last sc, 2 sc in last sc. Ch 1, turn.

Row 5: Sc across to last sc, 2 sc in last sc. Sl st in next ch-1 loop at end of row of star point. Ch 1, turn.

Rows 6–9: Repeat Rows 4 and 5 until there are 9 sc on row. At end of Row 9, sl st in joining st between star points. Sl st in the end of the next row of the next star point. Ch 1, turn.

Row 10: Skip 1 sc, sc in each sc to end (8 sc). Ch 1, turn.

Row 11: Skip 1 sc, sc in each sc to end (7 sc). Sl st in ch-1 loop at the end of Row 6 of next point, Ch 1, turn.

Row 12: Work as for Row 10 (6 sc).

Row 13: Work as for Row 11, making sl st in next ch-loop of point.

Rows 14–18: Work as for Rows 12 and 13 (1 sc remaining). Sl st in right side of sc at tip of next point. Ch 1 over tip, sl st in left side of same sc.

Next 5 Blocks: Repeat Rows 1–13 between each star point. At the end of the last block, join with sl st at right side of sc in star tip, ch 1 over tip, insert hook in beginning ch-1 of first block pull up a loop of Turquoise Print of complete sl st. Fasten off Large Orange Flower Print.

Border:

Rnd 1: Ch 1, sc in same space as joining, sc in the end of each row of Filler block to center point (Row 9). Work (sc across ends of rows to next center point, work 3 sc in end of this row) five times around, sc across row ends. Join with sl st in top of beginning ch-1.

Row 2: Ch 1, work (sc in each sc to center sc of 3-sc group at point, work 3 sc in this sc) around, sc in each sc to end. Join. Attach Small Orange Flower Print in last stitch. Fasten off Turquoise Print.

Row 3: Work as for Row 2. Attach Large Orange Flower Print. Fasten off Turquoise Print.

Rows 4–5: Work as for Row 2. Fasten off. Weave in end.

Log Cabin

APPROXIMATE SIZE: 28" x 22"

TOOLS: Size P crochet hook

GAUGE: 3 sc = 2"

STITCHES: Chain stitch (ch), Single crochet (sc), Slip stitch (sl st)

WIDTH OF STRIPS: 1⅛"

COLOR	FABRIC YARDAGE	COLOR	FABRIC YARDAGE
Block 1	¼ yard	Block 8	1½ yards
Block 2	¼ yard	Block 9	¾ yard
Block 3	⅜ yard	Block 10	1⅞ yards
Block 4	⅜ yard	Border 1	¾ yard
Block 5	¾ yard	Border 2	½ yard
Block 6	1¼ yards	Border 3	¾ yard
Block 7	1⅜ yards		

NOTE: Feel free to work as many rows for each block as desired. Work either an odd or even number of rows for each color block according to instructions to change colors. Turn rug and work blocks from center without sewing.

INSTRUCTIONS

Begin: With Block 1, ch 6.

Row 1: Sc in second ch from hook, sc in next 4 ch, ch 1, turn.

Rows 2–4: Sc in each sc across. Ch 1, turn at the end of each row. Attach Block 2 fabric in last stitch of Row 4. Fasten off Block 1 fabric. Ch 1, turn.

Block 2: Work 3 rows (or an odd number) as above. Attach Block 3 fabric in last stitch. Fasten off Block 2 fabric. Ch 1, turn to work across sides of blocks.

Log Cabin rug created by Jan Werner.

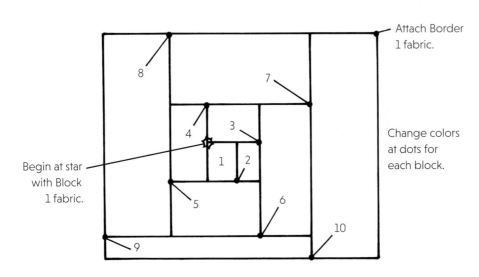

Attach Border 1 fabric.

Change colors at dots for each block.

Begin at star with Block 1 fabric.

Block 3: Work 5 rows:

Row 1: Sc in the end of each row (7 sc). Ch 1, turn.

Rows 2–5: Sc in each sc across. Ch 1, turn. Attach Block 4 fabric in last stitch. Fasten off Block 3 fabric. Ch 1, turn to work across ends of Block 3 rows.

Block 4: Work 5 rows:

Row 1: Sc in the end of each Block 3 row and across foundation chain of Block 1 (9 sc). Ch 1, turn.

Rows 2–5: Sc in each sc across. Ch 1, turn. Attach Block 5 fabric in last stitch. Fasten off Block 4. Ch 1, turn to work across ends of rows.

Block 5: Work 7 rows:

Row 1: Sc in the end of each Block 4, Block 1, and Block 2 row across (12 sc). Ch 1, turn.

Rows 2–7: Sc in each sc across. Ch 1, turn. Attach Block 6 fabric in last stitch. Fasten off Block 5. Ch 1, turn to work across ends of rows.

Block 6: Work 7 rows:

Row 1: Sc in the end of each Block 5 row, across last row of Block 2, and in the end of each Block 3 row. Ch 1, turn.

Rows 2–7: Sc in each sc across. Ch 1, turn. Attach Block 7 fabric in last stitch. Fasten off Block 6. Ch 1, turn to work across ends of rows.

Block 7: Work 9 rows:

Row 1: Sc in the end of each Block 6 row, across top of Block 3 block, and in end of each Block 4 row.

Rows 2–9: Sc in each sc across. Ch 1, turn. Attach Block 3 fabric in last stitch. Fasten off Block 7. Ch 1, turn to work across ends of rows.

Block 8: Work 9 rows:

Row 1: Sc in the end of each Block 7 row, across Block 4, and in end of each Block 5 row. Ch 1, turn.

Rows 2–9: Sc in each sc across. Ch 1, turn. Attach Block 9 fabric in last stitch. Fasten off Block 8. Ch 1, turn to work across ends of rows.

Block 9: Work 3 rows:

Row 1: Sc in the end of each row of Block 8, across Block 5, and in end of each Block 6 now. Ch 1, turn.

Rows 2–3: Sc in each sc across. Ch 1, turn. Attach Block 10 fabric in last stitch. Fasten off Block 9. Turn to work across ends of rows.

Block 10: Work 9 rows:

Row 1: Sc in the end of each Block 9 row, across Block 6, and in end of each Block 7 row. Ch 1, turn.

Rows 2–9: Attach Border 1 fabric in last stitch. Fasten off Block 10. Ch 1, turn to work across ends of rows.

Border:

Row 1: Work (sc in the end of each row or sc across side, work 3 sc in last row or sc) around. Join with sl st to top of beginning ch-1.

Row 2: Ch 1, work (sc in each sc to center sc of 3-sc corner group, work 3 sc in this sc) around. Join. Attach Border 3 fabric in last stitch. Fasten off Border 2 fabric.

Rows 3–4: Work as for Row 2. Fasten off. Weave in end.

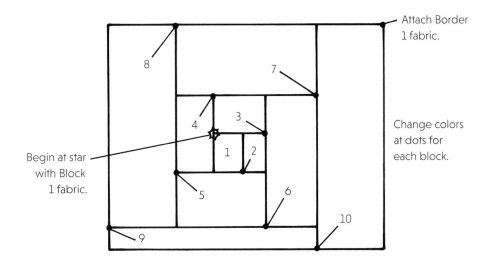

Striped

Striped rug
created by
Kathy E. Hellems.

APPROXIMATE SIZE: 16" x 21"

TOOLS: Size Q crochet hook

GAUGE: 3 sl st = 2"

STITCHES: Chain stitch (ch), Slip stitch (sl st), Double crochet (dc),
Half double crochet (hdc)

WIDTH OF STRIPS: 2¼"

COLOR	FABRIC YARDAGE
Flag Print	4 yards
Solid Blue	8⅔ yards
Stars Print	5 yards

INSTRUCTIONS

Begin: With Stars Print, ch 21.

Row 1: Make a sl st in the 2nd ch from hook, sl st in each of the next 19 ch, ch 1, turn.

Row 2: Sl st in each sl st across (20 sl st), ch 1, turn.

Rows 3–5: Repeat Row 2. Attach Flags Print in last stitch. Fasten off Stars Print.

Rows 6–10: Repeat Row 2. Attach Solid Blue in last stitch. Fasten off Flags Print.

Rows 11–15: Repeat Row 2. Attach Stars Print in last stitch. Fasten off Solid Blue.

Rows 16–20: Repeat Row 2. Attach Flags Print in last stitch. Fasten off Stars Print.

Rows 21–25: Repeat Row 2. Attach Solid Blue in last stitch. Fasten off Flags Print.

Rows 26–30: Repeat Row 2. Attach Stars Print in last stitch. Fasten off Solid Blue.

Rows 31–35: Repeat Row 2. Fasten off.

Border: Attach Solid Blue in the first stitch of Row 35. Ch 1, work *(sl st in each sl st across), 3 sl st in the 1st st on the side (for corner), sl st in the end of each of the next 33 rows, 3 sl st in the end of the row*. Repeat from * to * (118 sl st). Join with sl st in top of beginning ch-1.

Rnd 2: Ch 1 (first sl st), work sl st in each sl st across to center sl st of 3-sl st corner group, work 3 sl st in this sl st around. Sl st in the last sl st. Join. Attach Flags Print. Fasten off Solid Blue.

Note: 22 sl st across the end, 35 sl st across the sides.

Rnds 3–4: Repeat Row 2, adding 2 sl st on each side between corners. Do not fasten off.

Shell Border: Ch 1, sl st in next sl st, *work (hdc in next sl st, 2 dc in next sl st, hdc in next sl st, sl st in next sl st to corner. Work hdc in first sl st of corner group, 3 dc in center sl st, hdc in next sl st, sl st in next sl st*. Repeat * to * around – 43 shells. Join. Fasten off. Weave in end.

Heart with Twisted Loop Border

APPROXIMATE SIZE: 29" across x 21" high (excluding loop border)

TOOLS: Size Q crochet hook, rug needle

GAUGE: 4 sc = 3"

STITCHES: Chain stitch (ch), Slip stitch (sl st), Single crochet (sc)

WIDTH OF STRIPS: 2¼"

COLOR	FABRIC YARDAGE
White	4 yards
Coral	2 yards
Mint	4 yards

INSTRUCTIONS

Begin: With White, ch 22.

Rnd 1: Sc in 2nd ch from hook and in each of the next 9 ch. Skip next ch (dip). Sc in each of the next 9 ch, work 4 sc in last ch. Turn to work across other side of foundation chain. Sc in each of the next 9 ch, make 3 sc in next ch (tip), sc in each of the next 9 sc, work 2 sc in last ch – 46 sc. Join.

Rnd 2: Ch 1, sc in same space as joining, work 2 sc in next sc, sc in each of the next 8 sc, insert hook in next sc, pull up loop, insert hook in next sc, pull up loop, yarn over hook and pull through 3 loops on hook (decrease made), sc in each of the next 8 sc, work 2 sc in each of the 4 sc around end. Sc in each of the next 10 sc to center sc of 3-sc group at tip. Work 3 sc in this sc. Sc in each of the next 10 sc, work 2 sc in each of the next 2 sc – 55 sc. Join.

Rnd 3: Ch 1, sc in same space as joining, work 2 sc in each of the next 2 sc, sc in each of the next 19 sc, work 2 sc in each of the next 5 sc around end. Sc in each of the next 13 sc, work 3 sc in next sc, sc in each of the next 13 sc, work 2 sc in each of the next 2 sc – 67 sc. Join. Attach Mint. Fasten off White.

Rnd 4: Ch 1, sc in same space as joining, work 2 sc in each of the next 2 sc, sc in each of the next 12 sc, decrease over next 2 sc, sc in each of the next 11 sc, work 2 sc in each of the next 5 sc. Sc in each of the next 16 sc, work 3 sc in next sc, sc in each of the next 13 sc – 71 stitches.

Rnd 5: Ch 1, sc in each of the next 2 sc, work 2 sc in each of the next 2 sc, sc in each of the next 12 sc, decrease over next 2 sc. Sc in each of the next 11 sc, work 2 sc in each of the next 3 sc, sc in each of the next 22 sc, work 3 sc in next 2 sc, sc in each of the next 16 sc – 77 sc. Join. Attach Coral. Fasten off Mint.

Heart with Twisted Loop Border rug created by Sara Quintana.

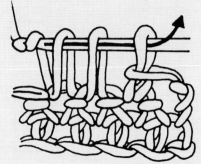

To decrease in sc, insert hook in st, draw up a loop, insert hook in next st, draw up a loop—3 loops on hook. Yarn over hook, draw through all 3 loops.

Heart with Twisted Loop Border *(continued)*

Rnd 6: Ch 1, sc in same space as joining, work 2 sc in each of the next 2 sc, sc in each of the next 16 sc, decrease over next 2 sc. Sc in each of the next 16 sc, work 2 sc in each of the next 3 sc, sc in each of the next 21 sc, work 3 sc in next 2 sc, sc in each of the next 20 sc – 91 sc. Join. Attach Mint. Fasten off Coral.

Rnd 7: Ch 1, sc in each of the 2 sc, work 2 sc in each of the next 2 sc, sc in each of the next 2 sc, work 2 sc in next sc. Sc in each of the next 14 sc, skip next sc, sc in each of the next 14 sc, work 2 sc in next sc, sc in each of the next 2 sc, work 2 sc in next 2 sc, sc in each of the next 24 sc. Work 3 sc in next sc, sc in each of the next 23 sc – 96 sc. Join.

Rnd 8: Ch 1, sc in each of the 6 sc, work 2 sc in each of the next 2 sc, sc in each of the next 14 sc, decrease over next 2 sc. Sc in each of the next 14 sc, work 2 sc in next sc, sc in each of the next 2 sc, work 2 sc in each of the next 2 sc, sc in each of the next 28 sc, work 3 sc in next sc, sc in each of the next 24 sc–102 sc. Join.

Rnd 9: Ch 1, sc in same space as joining, sc in each of the next 3 sc, work 2 sc in next sc, sc in each of the next 20 sc, skip next sc. Sc in each of the next 20 sc, work 2 sc in next sc, sc in each of the next 3 sc, work 2 sc in next sc, sc in each of the next 25 sc, work 3 sc in next sc, sc in each of the next 25 sc–106 sc. Join. Fasten off Mint. Weave in end.

Twisted Loop Border: With right side of rug facing, hold rug upside down and attach Coral in 3rd sc of tip (at left of center sc of group). * Hold loop on hook with finger to keep it from slipping from hook. Turn hook clockwise one complete turn. Ch 7. Carefully remove loop from hook and hold loop with other hand. Do not let chain untwist. Skip 2 sc. Insert hook from right side of rug to pull up loop from back, sl st. Repeat from * around – 36 loops. Join with sl st in last sc. Fasten off. Weave in end.

Use Leftover Fabrics to Create Fun and EASY Rugs

Turn colorful scraps into durable rugs! All you need are the foolproof and easy-to-follow instructions provided in this book, plus some fabric strips and a large crochet hook. You'll be amazed at how simple and fun it is to make beautiful rugs using inexpensive materials and supplies.

With gorgeous color photographs and clear, straightforward instructions, Suzanne McNeill presents 16 lovely projects to make with strips of fabric. Crafters of all ages and skill levels will enjoy using her simple crochet techniques. Discover how to update this traditional craft with endless possibilities of color and fabric combinations. Whether the pattern is square, rectangular, hexagonal, round, oval, or heart-shaped, each custom rag rug you make is sure to become an instant heirloom treasure.

- ■ 16 fun projects for making beautiful rugs from leftover fabric
- ■ Great ways to recycle old sheets, tablecloths, or curtains
- ■ Create warm and cozy accents for your home
- ■ Simple, easy-to-learn crochet techniques
- ■ Square, rectangular, hexagonal, round, oval, and heart-shaped patterns

ABOUT THE AUTHOR: Winner of the Craft and Hobby Association's Industry Achievement Award, Suzanne McNeill has been called "the Trendsetter" of arts and crafts. Dedicated to hands-on creativity, she constantly tests, experiments and invents something new and fun. As the author of more than 230 craft & hobby books, Suzanne's creative vision has placed her books on top of the trends for over 25 years.

No. 5476

0 23863 05476 8

Design Originals
an Imprint of Fox Chapel Publishing
www.d-originals.com

ISBN: 978-1-57421-918-0
EAN
51299
9 781574 219180